CHECKERBOARD BIOGRAPHY LIBRARY

U.S. PRESIDENTS

The
United States Presiden

BARACK OBAMA

ABDO Publishing Company

Tamara L. Britton

Visit us at
www.abdopublishing.com

Published by ABDO Publishing Company, PO Box 398166, Minneapolis, MN 55439.
Copyright © 2014 by Abdo Consulting Group, Inc. International copyrights reserved in all
countries. No part of this book may be reproduced in any form without written permission from the
publisher. The Checkerboard Library™ is a trademark and logo of ABDO Publishing Company.

Printed in the United States of America, North Mankato, Minnesota.
052013
092013

PRINTED ON RECYCLED PAPER

Cover Photo: Public Domain
Interior Photos: AP Images pp. 8, 9, 11, 14, 16, 17, 18, 19, 21, 22, 23; Corbis pp. 27, 28;
    Getty Images pp. 5, 15, 24, 25, 26, 29; Glow Images p. 12; Thinkstock p. 13

Editors: Rochelle Baltzer, Megan M. Gunderson
Art Direction: Neil Klinepier

Library of Congress Control Number: 2013904364

Cataloging-in-Publication Data

Britton, Tamara L.
 Barack Obama / Tamara L. Britton.
  p. cm. -- (The United States presidents)
 ISBN 978-1-61783-492-9
 Includes bibliographical references and index.
 1. Obama, Barack--Juvenile literature. 2. Presidents--United States--Biography--Juvenile literature.
 3. Racially mixed people--United States--Biography--Juvenile literature. I. Title.
 973.932/092--dc23
 [B]   2013904364

CONTENTS

Barack Obama 4

Timeline. 6

Did You Know? 7

Young Barry 8

School Days 10

The Power of Change. 12

Building Community. 14

Becoming a Lawyer 16

Finding a Purpose. 18

Senator Obama 20

Running for President 22

President Obama 24

Four More Years 28

Office of the President 30

Presidents and Their Terms 34

Glossary 38

Web Sites 39

Index 40

BARACK OBAMA

On November 20, 2008, Barack Obama was elected the forty-fourth U.S. president. It was a historic achievement. No other African American had ever held the office.

Obama began his career as a community organizer. Later, he went to law school. Then, he entered politics.

In the Illinois state senate, Obama sought to reform campaign finance laws. He also worked to expand education.

As a U.S. senator, Obama worked for alternative energy, **environmental** protection, and free trade. He also worked to reduce nuclear weapons.

During his first term, President Obama faced many challenges. He worked to end the wars in Iraq and Afghanistan. He also signed laws that helped the struggling **economy**. He extended health care to all. And, he improved children's **nutrition**.

In 2012, voters continued to believe in Obama. They reelected him for a second term.

TIMELINE

1961 - On August 4, Barack Hussein Obama Jr. was born in Honolulu, Hawaii.

1983 - Obama graduated from Columbia University in New York City, New York.

1985 - Obama moved to Chicago, Illinois, where he began working as a community organizer.

1990 - Obama was elected the first African-American president of the *Harvard Law Review*.

1991 - Obama graduated with honors from Harvard Law School in Cambridge, Massachusetts.

1992 - Obama married Michelle LaVaughn Robinson; he began teaching at the University of Chicago; Obama led Illinois Project VOTE.

1996 - Obama was elected to the Illinois state senate.

2004 - Obama won election to the U.S. Senate.

2008 - Obama became the Democratic nominee for U.S. president on August 27; on November 4, Obama defeated John McCain to win the presidential election.

2009 - On January 20, Obama took office as the forty-fourth U.S. president; Obama signed the American Recovery and Reinvestment Act on February 17.

2010 - In March, Obama signed the Patient Protection and Affordable Care Act; in April, Obama signed the Strategic Arms Reduction Treaty; troops withdrew from Iraq in August; Obama signed the Healthy Hunger-Free Kids Act in December.

2011 - Osama bin Laden was killed in Pakistan.

2012 - On November 6, President Obama defeated Mitt Romney to win a second term.

DID YOU KNOW?

The name *Barack* means "blessed" in the Swahili language.

When Obama entered the U.S. Senate in 2005, he was the only African-American senator. And, he was only the fifth African-American senator in U.S. history.

In 2009, Obama became the third U.S. president to win the Nobel Peace Prize. Theodore Roosevelt and Woodrow Wilson are the other two.

In 2009, Obama appointed the first Hispanic Justice to the U.S. Supreme Court. Sonia Sotomayor assumed office on August 8 of that year.

PRESIDENT OF THE
POTUS
UNITED STATES

YOUNG BARRY

Barack Hussein Obama Jr. was born on August 4, 1961, in Honolulu, Hawaii. As a boy, he was called Barry.

Barry was named after his father. Barack Obama Sr. was from Africa. He grew up in Alego, Kenya. He was a member of the Luo tribe.

In 1959, Barack Sr. became the first African student to attend the University of Hawaii in Honolulu. There, he was a business student. He studied **economics**.

Barack Obama Sr.

FAST FACTS

BORN - August 4, 1961
WIFE - Michelle LaVaughn Robinson
   (1964–)
CHILDREN - 2
POLITICAL PARTY - Democrat
AGE AT INAUGURATION - 47
YEARS SERVED - 2009–
VICE PRESIDENT - Joe Biden

8

Barry's mother was Stanley Ann Dunham. She was called Ann. Ann was born in Wichita, Kansas. She also attended the University of Hawaii. She studied **anthropology**.

In 1964, Barry's parents divorced. His father left Hawaii to study at Harvard University in Cambridge, Massachusetts. Later, he returned to Kenya.

Barry's mother soon remarried. His stepfather, Lolo Soetoro, was a student at

Barry and his mother, Ann

the University of Hawaii. He studied **geography**.

Lolo was from Indonesia. When Barry was six, he and his mother joined Lolo there. They settled in the capital city of Jakarta. There, Barry's sister Maya was born in 1970.

SCHOOL DAYS

In Indonesia, Ann worried about the quality of Barry's education. So every morning, she woke Barry up early. She taught him English lessons from a **correspondence course**.

When he was ten years old, Ann decided Barry would return to Hawaii for school. He lived with her parents in Honolulu. With their help, Barry earned a **scholarship** to attend Punahou School.

Punahou was Hawaii's most prestigious **preparatory school**. Only a few African-American students attended. Barry felt especially different because he had a white mother and a black father.

In 1972, Barry's mother returned to Hawaii to continue her education. That same year, Barack Sr. returned to Hawaii to visit. He and Barry went to a jazz concert. And, he spoke to the students at Barry's school about Kenya.

After a month, Barack Sr. left. Barry would not see him again. Barack Sr. died in a car accident in 1982.

When Barry was 14, his mother returned to Indonesia for further study. But Barry didn't want to be the new kid in school again. So, he stayed in Hawaii with his grandparents.

Barry was an average student. Sometimes he focused more on basketball than schoolwork! Yet he was very smart. Barry graduated from high school with **honors** in 1979.

Barry and his Punahou classmates on a field trip to Tokyo, Japan

THE POWER OF CHANGE

After high school, Obama moved to Los Angeles, California. There, he attended Occidental College. In college, Obama began to focus more on schoolwork than basketball.

At Occidental, Obama lived in this dorm room in Haines Hall.

Obama began keeping a journal. He also wrote poems. They were published in the school's **literary** magazine.

Obama also began to get involved in social issues. He began to consider how life is experienced by African Americans. And, he gave a speech at Occidental about problems in South Africa. Obama came to realize that words could be powerful tools for change.

Obama was exploring society and himself. He decided to attend college in a larger city. So in 1981, he transferred to Columbia University in New York City, New York.

Obama spent much time studying at Columbia's beautiful Butler Library.

At Columbia, Obama studied **political science**. He also continued to think about the ways racial differences affect communities. He grew convinced that **activism** was important in bringing about change.

Obama graduated from college in 1983. He then got an office job. Yet, he wanted to work in community service. Obama sent out letters across the United States seeking a job. But no one replied.

BUILDING COMMUNITY

Jerry Kellman hired Obama for his first community service job. He became an important mentor.

One day, Obama was at the New York Public Library. He was reading newspapers to find ads for community service jobs. He saw one for a position in Chicago, Illinois.

The job was for an African-American community organizer. The work was in the city's South Side neighborhoods. Obama applied and got the job!

In 1985, Obama moved to Chicago's South Side. At one time, the steel industry had employed many people there. But the steel mills closed. Jobs were few. Some people turned to drugs or joined gangs. Obama's organization helped people find new jobs.

Obama's work also took him to the area's public housing projects. At Altgeld Gardens, he listened to the residents tell their stories. He learned about the problems they faced. Obama then helped them work with city leaders to improve their community.

Obama believed community involvement could improve lives. He enjoyed his work. But it was not easy. Government officials often hesitated to change the way things were done. So, Obama felt that laws and policies must also change. After three years, he returned to school to study law.

Altgeld Gardens was a stop on the Underground Railroad.

BECOMING A LAWYER

In 1988, Obama entered Harvard Law School in Cambridge, Massachusetts. The following year, he was an **intern** at Chicago's Sidley Austin LLP law firm. There, he met Harvard Law School graduate Michelle LaVaughn Robinson. The two stayed in touch when Obama returned to school.

At Harvard, Obama showed strong leadership skills. He was also a good writer and editor. So in 1990,

A monument in their Chicago neighborhood marks the spot where the Obamas first kissed.

Obama was elected president of the *Harvard Law Review*. He beat out 19 other students for the job. Obama was the first African American to hold this position.

The *Harvard Law Review* is published monthly during the school year. Obama spent more than 40 hours a week managing this tight schedule. He also supervised the journal's 80 editors.

Obama thought privileged people should do work that benefits the common good. He also supported **affirmative action** as a way to create **diversity**. With Obama in charge, writers with different beliefs knew they would all have a voice.

Michelle, Malia, Barack, and Sasha Obama

Obama graduated from law school with **honors** in 1991. Then, he moved back to Chicago. On October 3, 1992, he and Michelle were married. The Obamas would go on to have two daughters. Malia Ann was born in 1998. Natasha, called Sasha, was born in 2001.

FINDING A PURPOSE

In 1992, Obama began teaching **constitutional** law at the University of Chicago. He also worked at the Miner, Barnhill and Galland law firm. Obama's cases involved voting rights and housing and employment **discrimination**.

Obama continued to work in his community. He served on the boards of the Woods Fund and the Joyce Foundation. These groups gave money to community organizations.

Obama also led Illinois Project VOTE in 1992. This organization worked to get more Hispanics and African Americans involved in the election process. Obama's efforts helped sign up more than 100,000 voters.

Obama had been gaining national attention since law school. He had also continued writing. Obama's first book came

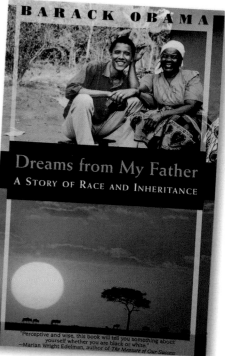

The first edition of Obama's first book

from writing about his life and struggles with racial identity. *Dreams from My Father: A Story of Race and Inheritance* was published in 1995.

Obama won a Grammy Award for the audio version of his second book, The Audacity of Hope.

SENATOR OBAMA

In 1996, Obama ran for the Illinois state senate as a **Democrat**. He won the election! He took office on January 8, 1997.

In the senate, Obama was chairman of the Public Health and Welfare Committee. He worked to increase funding for preventing and treating AIDS. He also worked to reduce racial **profiling**.

Senator Obama helped pass the Earned Income Tax Credit. This provided tax cuts for Illinois families. He also worked to expand early childhood education. Reform of campaign finance laws was another goal.

In 2000, Obama ran for the U.S. House of Representatives. Democrat Bobby Rush held the seat. Obama lost in the **primary** election.

Even so, Obama remained committed to his goals. In 2004, he ran for the U.S. Senate. He easily won the Democratic primary.

In November, Obama defeated **Republican** Alan Keyes. He took office on January 3, 2005.

Senator Obama served on the Foreign Relations and Veterans Affairs Committees. He also sat on the **Environment** and Public Works Committee. Obama supported alternative energy. He voted to strengthen environmental protection and frcc trade. He cosponsored a bill to reduce nuclear weapons. And, he opposed the war in Iraq.

In 2003, Illinois senator Obama argued for driver's licenses for undocumented immigrants. This became law in Illinois in 2013.

RUNNING FOR PRESIDENT

Obama at the 2004 DNC in Boston

Obama gained national attention during his U.S. Senate campaign. Then on July 27, 2004, he spoke at the **Democratic National Convention (DNC)** in Boston, Massachusetts.

In his speech, Obama spoke of the nation's history and **diversity**. He talked about suffering he had seen. He called on Americans to unite to solve these problems.

John McCain and Sarah Palin

Many Americans wondered if Obama planned to run for president. On February 10, 2007, he announced he would. He faced strong competition. New York senator Hillary Rodham Clinton won important early **primaries**.

But in the end, Obama won more. On August 27, 2008, he became the **Democratic** Party's nominee for president. He chose Delaware senator Joe Biden as his **running mate**.

In the general election, Obama and Biden faced off against **Republican** senator John McCain of Arizona. McCain's running mate was Alaska governor Sarah Palin.

Obama and McCain both ran tough campaigns. Voters looked to them for answers to the struggling **economy**. Many wanted an end to the wars in Iraq and Afghanistan.

On November 4, 2008, Americans went to the polls. They chose Barack Obama to be the nation's forty-fourth president. He took office on January 20, 2009. That day, Obama became the first African-American president in U.S. history.

PRESIDENT OBAMA

President Obama took immediate action. On February 17, 2009, he signed the American Recovery and Reinvestment Act. The bill provided for unemployment benefits, education, and other programs.

In Congress, **Democrats** and **Republicans** sought ways to improve the nation's health care. To this end, the president signed the Patient Protection and Affordable Care Act in March 2010. It gave health coverage to 32 million uninsured Americans.

Obama continued his focus on limiting nuclear weapons. On April 8, he signed the Strategic Arms Reduction Treaty with Russian president Dmitry Medvedev.

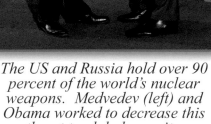

The US and Russia hold over 90 percent of the world's nuclear weapons. Medvedev (left) and Obama worked to decrease this threat to global security.

SUPREME COURT APPOINTMENTS

SONIA SOTOMAYOR - 2009
ELENA KAGAN - 2010

With the help of American Recovery and Reinvestment Act funds, Chicago's Exelon City Solar Plant was built. It is the nation's largest urban solar power station.

On April 20, there was an explosion at an oil well in the Gulf of Mexico. Eleven workers were killed. Millions of gallons of oil spilled into the gulf. The disaster presented problems for gulf workers, wildlife, and the **environment**. The president created a group that included both **Democrats** and **Republicans**. He asked them to determine how to prevent a similar accident.

First Lady Michelle Obama has made improving children's nutrition her priority.

On December 13, 2010, Obama signed the Healthy Hunger-Free Kids Act. This law improved the national School Lunch Program. Only whole grains could be served to students. And, lunches had to include twice the fruits and vegetables as in the past.

Obama also worked to continue improving the nation's **economy**. On December 17, the president signed another bill. It gave some Americans tax cuts. It extended unemployment insurance for others.

The ongoing wars remained a key issue. Combat troops withdrew from Iraq on August 31, 2010. But more work needed to be done in Afghanistan. So, the president sent more troops.

Then on May 2, 2011, President Obama ordered a secret raid. Troops stormed a house in Pakistan. There, they killed terrorist leader Osama bin Laden.

That fall, the federal government was nearing its debt ceiling. Congress debated on how to balance the budget. **Republicans** wanted to cut spending. **Democrats** wanted to increase spending. On August 2, 2011, Obama signed a law to raise the debt limit. It also called for spending cuts over a ten-year period.

President Obama's Cabinet

January 20, 2009–

- **STATE –** Hillary Rodham Clinton
  - John Kerry (from February 1, 2013)
- **TREASURY –** Timothy F. Geithner
  - Jacob J. Lew (from February 27, 2013)
- **DEFENSE –** Robert M. Gates
  - Leon E. Panetta (from July 1, 2011)
  - Chuck Hagel (from February 27, 2013)

- **ATTORNEY GENERAL –** Eric H. Holder Jr.
- **INTERIOR –** Kenneth L. Salazar
  - Sally Jewell (from April 10, 2012)
- **AGRICULTURE –** Thomas J. Vilsack
- **COMMERCE –** Gary F. Locke
  - John E. Bryson (from October 21, 2011)
  - Rebecca Blank (acting from June 21, 2012)
  - Cameron F. Kerry (acting from June 1, 2013)
  - Penny Pritzker (from June 26, 2013)
- **LABOR –** Hilda L. Solis
  - Seth D. Harris (acting from January 22, 2013)
  - Tom Perez (from July 23, 2013)
- **HEALTH AND HUMAN SERVICES –** Kathleen Sebelius
- **HOUSING AND URBAN DEVELOPMENT –**
  - Shaun L.S. Donovan
- **TRANSPORTATION –** Ray LaHood
  - Anthony Foxx (from July 2, 2013)
- **ENERGY –** Steven Chu
  - Ernest Moniz (from May 21, 2013)
- **EDUCATION –** Arne Duncan
- **VETERANS AFFAIRS –** Eric K. Shinseki
- **HOMELAND SECURITY –** Janet A. Napolitano
  - Rand Beers (acting from September 6, 2013)

*Chuck Hagel is the first Vietnam War
veteran to serve as secretary of defense.*

Four More Years

The president's first term was filled with achievements. But the **economy** continued to struggle. And each year, the federal government spent more than it took in.

As the 2012 election approached, **Republicans** claimed Obama was not effective. **Democrats** claimed the president had gained many problems when he took office. He needed more time to solve them.

On August 28, 2012, Republicans nominated former Massachusetts governor Willard "Mitt" Romney as their candidate. He chose Wisconsin congressman Paul Ryan as his **running mate**. To balance the budget, Romney wanted to cut spending. He also wanted to change Medicare and Social Security.

On November 6, 2012, Americans let their voices be heard. President Obama and Vice President Biden received

Mitt Romney (left) *and Paul Ryan*

332 **Electoral College** votes. Romney and Ryan came away with 206. President Obama had won reelection.

Obama's second term began January 21, 2013. He had many aims. These included reducing the federal budget deficit. He also wanted to reduce oil imports and create jobs. And, gun control was a key goal. These were challenging tasks. But Americans showed they had confidence in their president.

President Obama and his family greet supporters on the night of his reelection.

OFFICE OF THE PRESIDENT

BRANCHES OF GOVERNMENT

The U.S. government is divided into three branches. They are the executive, legislative, and judicial branches. This division is called a separation of powers. Each branch has some power over the others. This is called a system of checks and balances.

EXECUTIVE BRANCH

The executive branch enforces laws. It is made up of the president, the vice president, and the president's cabinet. The president represents the United States around the world. He or she oversees relations with other countries and signs treaties. The president signs bills into law and appoints officials and federal judges. He or she also leads the military and manages government workers.

LEGISLATIVE BRANCH

The legislative branch makes laws, maintains the military, and regulates trade. It also has the power to declare war. This branch consists of the Senate and the House of Representatives. Together, these two houses make up Congress. Each state has two senators. A state's population determines the number of representatives it has.

JUDICIAL BRANCH

The judicial branch interprets laws. It consists of district courts, courts of appeals, and the Supreme Court. District courts try cases. If a person disagrees with a trial's outcome, he or she may appeal. If the courts of appeals support the ruling, a person may appeal to the Supreme Court. The Supreme Court also makes sure that laws follow the U.S. Constitution.

QUALIFICATIONS FOR OFFICE

To be president, a person must meet three requirements. A candidate must be at least 35 years old and a natural-born U.S. citizen. He or she must also have lived in the United States for at least 14 years.

ELECTORAL COLLEGE

The U.S. presidential election is an indirect election. Voters from each state choose electors to represent them in the Electoral College. The number of electors from each state is based on population. Each elector has one electoral vote. Electors are pledged to cast their vote for the candidate who receives the highest number of popular votes in their state. A candidate must receive the majority of Electoral College votes to win.

TERM OF OFFICE

Each president may be elected to two four-year terms. Sometimes, a president may only be elected once. This happens if he or she served more than two years of the previous president's term.

The presidential election is held on the Tuesday after the first Monday in November. The president is sworn in on January 20 of the following year. At that time, he or she takes the oath of office:

I do solemnly swear (or affirm) that I will faithfully execute the office of President of the United States, and will to the best of my ability, preserve, protect and defend the Constitution of the United States.

LINE OF SUCCESSION

The Presidential Succession Act of 1947 defines who becomes president if the president cannot serve. The vice president is first in the line of succession. Next are the Speaker of the House and the President Pro Tempore of the Senate. If none of these individuals is able to serve, the office falls to the president's cabinet members. They would take office in the order in which each department was created:

| Secretary of State |
| Secretary of the Treasury |
| Secretary of Defense |
| Attorney General |
| Secretary of the Interior |
| Secretary of Agriculture |
| Secretary of Commerce |
| Secretary of Labor |
| Secretary of Health and Human Services |
| Secretary of Housing and Urban Development |
| Secretary of Transportation |
| Secretary of Energy |
| Secretary of Education |
| Secretary of Veterans Affairs |
| Secretary of Homeland Security |

BENEFITS

- While in office, the president receives a salary of $400,000 each year. He or she lives in the White House and has 24-hour Secret Service protection.

- The president may travel on a Boeing 747 jet called Air Force One. The airplane can accommodate 70 passengers. It has kitchens, a dining room, sleeping areas, and a conference room. It also has fully equipped offices with the latest communications systems. Air Force One can fly halfway around the world before needing to refuel. It can even refuel in flight!

- If the president wishes to travel by car, he or she uses Cadillac One. Cadillac One is a Cadillac Deville. It has been modified with heavy armor and communications systems. The president takes Cadillac One along when visiting other countries if secure transportation will be needed.

- The president also travels on a helicopter called Marine One. Like the presidential car, Marine One accompanies the president when traveling abroad if necessary.

- Sometimes, the president needs to get away and relax with family and friends. Camp David is the official presidential retreat. It is located in the cool, wooded mountains in Maryland. The U.S. Navy maintains the retreat, and the U.S. Marine Corps keeps it secure. The camp offers swimming, tennis, golf, and hiking.

- When the president leaves office, he or she receives Secret Service protection for ten more years. He or she also receives a yearly pension of $191,300 and funding for office space, supplies, and staff.

PRESIDENTS AND THEIR TERMS

PRESIDENT	PARTY	TOOK OFFICE	LEFT OFFICE	TERMS SERVED	VICE PRESIDENT
George Washington	None	April 30, 1789	March 4, 1797	Two	John Adams
John Adams	Federalist	March 4, 1797	March 4, 1801	One	Thomas Jefferson
Thomas Jefferson	Democratic-Republican	March 4, 1801	March 4, 1809	Two	Aaron Burr, George Clinton
James Madison	Democratic-Republican	March 4, 1809	March 4, 1817	Two	George Clinton, Elbridge Gerry
James Monroe	Democratic-Republican	March 4, 1817	March 4, 1825	Two	Daniel D. Tompkins
John Quincy Adams	Democratic-Republican	March 4, 1825	March 4, 1829	One	John C. Calhoun
Andrew Jackson	Democrat	March 4, 1829	March 4, 1837	Two	John C. Calhoun, Martin Van Buren
Martin Van Buren	Democrat	March 4, 1837	March 4, 1841	One	Richard M. Johnson
William H. Harrison	Whig	March 4, 1841	April 4, 1841	Died During First Term	John Tyler
John Tyler	Whig	April 6, 1841	March 4, 1845	Completed Harrison's Term	Office Vacant
James K. Polk	Democrat	March 4, 1845	March 4, 1849	One	George M. Dallas
Zachary Taylor	Whig	March 5, 1849	July 9, 1850	Died During First Term	Millard Fillmore

PRESIDENT	PARTY	TOOK OFFICE	LEFT OFFICE	TERMS SERVED	VICE PRESIDENT
Millard Fillmore	Whig	July 10, 1850	March 4, 1853	Completed Taylor's Term	Office Vacant
Franklin Pierce	Democrat	March 4, 1853	March 4, 1857	One	William R.D. King
James Buchanan	Democrat	March 4, 1857	March 4, 1861	One	John C. Breckinridge
Abraham Lincoln	Republican	March 4, 1861	April 15, 1865	Served One Term, Died During Second Term	Hannibal Hamlin, Andrew Johnson
Andrew Johnson	Democrat	April 15, 1865	March 4, 1869	Completed Lincoln's Second Term	Office Vacant
Ulysses S. Grant	Republican	March 4, 1869	March 4, 1877	Two	Schuyler Colfax, Henry Wilson
Rutherford B. Hayes	Republican	March 3, 1877	March 4, 1881	One	William A. Wheeler
James A. Garfield	Republican	March 4, 1881	September 19, 1881	Died During First Term	Chester Arthur
Chester Arthur	Republican	September 20, 1881	March 4, 1885	Completed Garfield's Term	Office Vacant
Grover Cleveland	Democrat	March 4, 1885	March 4, 1889	One	Thomas A. Hendricks
Benjamin Harrison	Republican	March 4, 1889	March 4, 1893	One	Levi P. Morton
Grover Cleveland	Democrat	March 4, 1893	March 4, 1897	One	Adlai E. Stevenson
William McKinley	Republican	March 4, 1897	September 14, 1901	Served One Term, Died During Second Term	Garret A. Hobart, Theodore Roosevelt

PRESIDENT	PARTY	TOOK OFFICE	LEFT OFFICE	TERMS SERVED	VICE PRESIDENT
Theodore Roosevelt	Republican	September 14, 1901	March 4, 1909	Completed McKinley's Second Term, Served One Term	Office Vacant, Charles Fairbanks
William Taft	Republican	March 4, 1909	March 4, 1913	One	James S. Sherman
Woodrow Wilson	Democrat	March 4, 1913	March 4, 1921	Two	Thomas R. Marshall
Warren G. Harding	Republican	March 4, 1921	August 2, 1923	Died During First Term	Calvin Coolidge
Calvin Coolidge	Republican	August 3, 1923	March 4, 1929	Completed Harding's Term, Served One Term	Office Vacant, Charles Dawes
Herbert Hoover	Republican	March 4, 1929	March 4, 1933	One	Charles Curtis
Franklin D. Roosevelt	Democrat	March 4, 1933	April 12, 1945	Served Three Terms, Died During Fourth Term	John Nance Garner, Henry A. Wallace, Harry S. Truman
Harry S. Truman	Democrat	April 12, 1945	January 20, 1953	Completed Roosevelt's Fourth Term, Served One Term	Office Vacant, Alben Barkley
Dwight D. Eisenhower	Republican	January 20, 1953	January 20, 1961	Two	Richard Nixon
John F. Kennedy	Democrat	January 20, 1961	November 22, 1963	Died During First Term	Lyndon B. Johnson
Lyndon B. Johnson	Democrat	November 22, 1963	January 20, 1969	Completed Kennedy's Term, Served One Term	Office Vacant, Hubert H. Humphrey
Richard Nixon	Republican	January 20, 1969	August 9, 1974	Completed First Term, Resigned During Second Term	Spiro T. Agnew, Gerald Ford

PRESIDENTS 26–37, 1901–1974

PRESIDENT	PARTY	TOOK OFFICE	LEFT OFFICE	TERMS SERVED	VICE PRESIDENT
Gerald Ford	Republican	August 9, 1974	January 20, 1977	Completed Nixon's Second Term	Nelson A. Rockefeller
Jimmy Carter	Democrat	January 20, 1977	January 20, 1981	One	Walter Mondale
Ronald Reagan	Republican	January 20, 1981	January 20, 1989	Two	George H.W. Bush
George H.W. Bush	Republican	January 20, 1989	January 20, 1993	One	Dan Quayle
Bill Clinton	Democrat	January 20, 1993	January 20, 2001	Two	Al Gore
George W. Bush	Republican	January 20, 2001	January 20, 2009	Two	Dick Cheney
Barack Obama	Democrat	January 20, 2009			Joe Biden

"We do not believe that in this country, freedom is reserved for the lucky, or happiness for the few." Barack Obama

WRITE TO THE PRESIDENT

You may write to the president at:

**The White House
1600 Pennsylvania Avenue NW
Washington, DC 20500**

You may e-mail the president at:
comments@whitehouse.gov

GLOSSARY

activism - a practice that emphasizes direct action in support of or in opposition to an issue that causes disagreement.

affirmative action - the practice of improving opportunities for education and employment for groups who have been treated unfairly in the past.

anthropology - the study of the beginnings, development, and behaviors of humans and their ancestors.

constitutional - something relating to or following the laws of a constitution. A constitution is the laws that govern a country or a state.

correspondence course - a class given by mail instead of in a classroom.

Democrat - a member of the Democratic political party. Democrats believe in social change and strong government.

Democratic National Convention (DNC) - a national meeting held every four years during which the Democratic Party chooses its candidates for president and vice president.

discrimination (dihs-krih-muh-NAY-shuhn) - unfair treatment based on factors such as a person's race, religion, or gender.

diversity - having people of different races or cultures in an organization.

economy - the way a nation uses its money, goods, and natural resources. Economics is the science of this.

Electoral College - the group of representatives that elects the U.S. president and vice president by casting electoral votes. Each state has a certain number of representatives, or electors, based on population. Electors cast their votes for the candidate who received the most popular votes in their state.

environment - all the surroundings that affect the growth and well-being of a living thing.

geography - the science of the location of things on Earth and their effects on one another.

honors - special credit given to a student for above-average work.

intern - an advanced student or graduate gaining supervised practical experience in his or her field.

literary - of or relating to books or literature.

nutrition - that which promotes growth, provides energy, repairs body tissues, and maintains life.

political science - the study of government and politics.

preparatory school - a typically private school that prepares students for college.

primary - a method of selecting candidates to run for public office. A political party holds an election among its own members to select the party members who will represent it in the coming general election.

profiling - the act of suspecting or targeting a person based on behavior or observed characteristics, such as race.

Republican - a member of the Republican political party. Republicans are conservative and believe in small government.

running mate - a candidate running for a lower-rank position on an election ticket, especially the candidate for vice president.

scholarship - a gift of money to help a student pay for instruction.

WEB SITES

To learn more about Barack Obama, visit ABDO Publishing Company online. Web sites about Barack Obama are featured on our Book Links page. These links are routinely monitored and updated to provide the most current information available.

www.abdopublishing.com

INDEX

A

Afghanistan, War in 4, 23, 26

American Recovery and Reinvestment Act 24

B

Biden, Joe 23, 28

bin Laden, Osama 26

birth 8

C

childhood 8, 9, 10, 11

Clinton, Hillary Rodham 23

community organizer 4, 13, 14, 15, 18

D

debt ceiling debate 26

Democratic National Convention 22

Democratic Party 20, 23, 24, 25, 26, 28

Dreams from My Father: A Story of Race and Inheritance 18, 19

E

Earned Income Tax Credit 20

economy 4, 23, 26, 28, 29

education 4, 10, 11, 12, 13, 15, 16, 17, 18

Environment and Public Works Committee 21

F

family 8, 9, 10, 11, 16, 17

federal budget deficit 28, 29

Foreign Relations Committee 21

G

Gulf of Mexico oil spill 25

H

Harvard Law Review 16, 17

health care 4, 24

Healthy Hunger-Free Kids Act 26

hobbies 11, 12

House of Representatives, U.S. 20

I

Illinois Project VOTE 18

Illinois state senate 4, 20

inauguration 23, 29

Iraq War 4, 21, 23, 26

K

Keyes, Alan 20

M

McCain, John 23

Medvedev, Dmitry 24

P

Palin, Sarah 23

Patient Protection and Affordable Care Act 24

Public Health and Welfare Committee 20

R

Republican Party 20, 23, 24, 25, 26, 28

Romney, Willard "Mitt" 28, 29

Rush, Bobby 20

Ryan, Paul 28, 29

S

Senate, U.S. 4, 20, 21, 22

Strategic Arms Reduction Treaty 24

V

Veterans Affairs Committee 21